FREEDOM

From The President to Marshal Stalin

The appointment of General
Eisenhower to command of
Overlord operation has been
decided upon.

Roosevelt

Cairo, Dec. 7. 43

Dear Eisenhower, I thought you
might like to have this as a memento.
It was written very hurriedly by me as the
final meeting broke up yesterday, the
President signing it immediately.

W.S.C.

FREEDOM

Reproductions of 26 significant documents, from the
Declaration of Independence through the United Nations
Charter, with a brief historical background of each

by Wilma Pitchford Hays

Coward-McCann, Inc.   New York

Seventh Impression

Library of Congress Catalog Card Number: 58-12118

MANUFACTURED IN THE UNITED STATES OF AMERICA

The photographs for the facsimile reproductions in this book were made by Peter A. Juley & Son and Stephen T. Syrotiak, Jr.

Designed by Polly Cameron

Clues to Reading the Documents

1. If you have a magnifying glass, you can read even the small print in the photographs of the original documents. Notice that some words were spelled differently than we spell them now. Also the letter "s" looked like the letter "f."

2. If your school has an opaque projector, this book can be placed in it. The photographs can be projected in large size onto a screen for the entire class to see.

3. The brief true stories told here give you high points in America's struggle for freedoms. If you go on and read more about your country's past, you can understand her future better.

The *Freedom Train* which traveled through the United States about ten years ago, and stopped at 300 cities, exhibited the documents seen in this book as well as many other important documents.

Freedom Shrines, which have been placed in some schools and libraries by local members of the National Exchange Clubs, also show photographs of these papers.

The original documents (except for those listed below), are in the National Archives at Washington, D. C. Jefferson's *Rough Draft of the Declaration of Independence* and the *Gettysburg Address* are in the Library of Congress at Washington, D. C. *John Paul Jones' Letter* belongs to the U.S. Naval Academy Museum at Annapolis. *The Star-Spangled Banner* belongs to the Walters Art Gallery at Baltimore. *Lee's Letter* is at Washington and Lee University, Lexington, Va. *Agreement for Invasion of Western Europe* is in the Franklin D. Roosevelt Library at Hyde Park, N.Y. *Selection of General Eisenhower as Commander of "Overlord"* belongs to President Eisenhower. *McAuliffe's Christmas Message* belongs to General McAuliffe. The *United Nations Charter* is in the State Department in Washington, D. C.

Contents
1776 – 1945

1. Thomas Jefferson's Rough Draft of the Declaration of Independence

This rough draft of the Declaration of Independence is not a neat paper. For that very reason, it shows how hard its writers worked on it.

Before a committee could even be appointed to write the Declaration, Congress had to vote a resolution for independence. One story about the resolution reminds Americans *how very important the vote of even one man or woman can be.*

One of Delaware's three delegates was against the resolution and two were for it. One of these two, Caesar Rodney, was very ill in his home eighty miles from Philadelphia, where the Congress met. Mr. Rodney received a letter telling him that the vote for independence was to be taken and Delaware would be tied unless he could be present.

The sick man left his bed and rode horseback all night through a storm of wind and rain. The next day he reached the Congress just as it was being called to order. Delaware's vote was called and the sick man managed to rise and say, "I vote for independence." Thus the colonies voted unanimously for the resolution for freedom.

Thomas Jefferson, thirty-three years old, was asked to write the important paper which declared that the United States of America was free from English rule. Young as he was, Jefferson had gained the respect of the colonists during the troubled years when they were deciding to set up a free and independent government. Jefferson was a student of government, science, literature and composition. The members of the committee felt that he could choose the right words to express the desire for liberty.

Besides Jefferson, who was from Virginia, four others were appointed to the committee to prepare the document. They were John Adams of Massachusetts, Benjamin Franklin of Pennsylvania, Roger Sherman of Connecticut and Robert R. Livingston of New York.

When Jefferson finished writing the Declaration, he asked the other members to read it and suggest any changes they felt should be made. In the margin, changes were written in by Benjamin Franklin and John Adams in their own handwriting. Jefferson himself made changes as he studied, again and again, the best words to guarantee to all future Americans the right to life, liberty and the pursuit of happiness.

The Declaration was then presented to Congress. It was debated and Congress voted additional changes. Finally this rough draft was ready to be copied and became the Declaration of Independence as it is today.

A Declaration by the Representatives of the UNITED STATES OF AMERICA, in General Congress assembled.

When in the course of human events it becomes necessary for one people to dissolve the political bands which have connected them with another, and to assume among the powers of the earth the separate and equal station to which the laws of nature & of nature's god entitle them, a decent respect to the opinions of mankind requires that they should declare the causes which impel them to the separation.

We hold these truths to be self-evident; that all men are created equal, that they are endowed by their creator with inherent & inalienable rights; that among these are life, & liberty, & the pursuit of happiness; that to secure these rights, governments are instituted among men, deriving their just powers from the consent of the governed; that whenever any form of government becomes destructive of these ends, it is the right of the people to alter or to abolish it, & to institute new government, laying it's foundation on such principles & organising it's powers in such form, as to them shall seem most likely to effect their safety & happiness. prudence indeed will dictate that governments long established should not be changed for light & transient causes: and accordingly all experience hath shewn that mankind are more disposed to suffer while evils are sufferable, than to right themselves by abolishing the forms to which they are accustomed. but when a long train of abuses & usurpations [begun at a distinguished period, &] pursuing invariably the same object, evinces a design to reduce them under absolute despotism, it is their right, it is their duty, to throw off such government & to provide new guards for their future security. such has been the patient sufferance of these colonies; & such is now the necessity which constrains them to alter their former systems of government. the history of the present king of Great Britain is a history of unremitting injuries and usurpations, [among which appears no solitary fact to contradict the uniform tenor of the rest, but all have] in direct object the establishment of an absolute tyranny over these states. to prove this, let facts be submitted to a candid world, [for the truth of which we pledge a faith yet unsullied by falsehood.]

2. The Unanimous Declaration of the Thirteen United States of America, July 4, 1776

Here is the official text, adopted by the Congress and precious to every American since it declares our right to freedom. The long second paragraph sets forth the natural rights of every person. Most of the remainder is a list of the injustices suffered by the colonists and the reasons for the break with England. The last lines pledge the lives, fortunes and sacred honor of the signers in support of this declaration.

Look at the signatures. Every man who signed for freedom risked his life, the lives of his family and the destruction of his home and business; and he knew what he risked. Great Britain had declared every Patriot a traitor to be hanged if he were caught. The United States of America was small and had no trained army to protect the signers. A man must have the greatest courage to take up the quill pen and sign this paper. Yet here are their names, written clear and strong.

Most of the signers were young men. A few, like Benjamin Franklin and Stephen Hopkins, were older. Notice how unevenly Stephen Hopkins' name is written. He said as he signed, "My hand shakes, but my heart does not."

Later many of the signers suffered the loss of their homes by fire. Their families were put in prison and some died because they dared to sign for freedom.

Most of those who lived continued to serve their country for many years. Several signers later became President of the United States. (Do you know which ones they are?)

Exactly fifty years after signing the Declaration for freedom, two of the signers died on the same day, the Fourth of July, 1826. They were Thomas Jefferson and John Adams.

IN CONGRESS, JULY 4, 1776.

The unanimous Declaration of the thirteen united States of America.

When in the Course of human events, it becomes necessary for one people to dissolve the political bands which have connected them with another, and to assume among the powers of the earth, the separate and equal station to which the Laws of Nature and of Nature's God entitle them, a decent respect to the opinions of mankind requires that they should declare the causes which impel them to the separation. — We hold these truths to be self-evident, that all men are created equal, that they are endowed by their Creator with certain unalienable Rights, that among these are Life, Liberty and the pursuit of Happiness. — That to secure these rights, Governments are instituted among Men, deriving their just powers from the consent of the governed, — That whenever any Form of Government becomes destructive of these ends, it is the Right of the People to alter or to abolish it, and to institute new Government, laying its foundation on such principles and organizing its powers in such form, as to them shall seem most likely to effect their Safety and Happiness. Prudence, indeed, will dictate that Governments long established should not be changed for light and transient causes; and accordingly all experience hath shewn, that mankind are more disposed to suffer, while evils are sufferable, than to right themselves by abolishing the forms to which they are accustomed. But when a long train of abuses and usurpations, pursuing invariably the same Object evinces a design to reduce them under absolute Despotism, it is their right, it is their duty, to throw off such Government, and to provide new Guards for their future security. — Such has been the patient sufferance of these Colonies; and such is now the necessity which constrains them to alter their former Systems of Government. The history of the present King of Great Britain is a history of repeated injuries and usurpations, all having in direct object the establishment of an absolute Tyranny over these States. To prove this, let Facts be submitted to a candid world. —

He has refused his Assent to Laws, the most wholesome and necessary for the public good. — He has forbidden his Governors to pass Laws of immediate and pressing importance, unless suspended in their operation till his Assent should be obtained; and when so suspended, he has utterly neglected to attend to them. — He has refused to pass other Laws for the accommodation of large districts of people, unless those people would relinquish the right of Representation in the Legislature, a right inestimable to them and formidable to tyrants only. — He has called together legislative bodies at places unusual, uncomfortable, and distant from the depository of their Public Records, for the sole purpose of fatiguing them into compliance with his measures. — He has dissolved Representative Houses repeatedly, for opposing with manly firmness his invasions on the rights of the people. — He has refused for a long time, after such dissolutions, to cause others to be elected; whereby the Legislative powers, incapable of Annihilation, have returned to the People at large for their exercise; the State remaining in the mean time exposed to all the dangers of invasion from without, and convulsions within. — He has endeavoured to prevent the population of these States; for that purpose obstructing the Laws for Naturalization of Foreigners; refusing to pass others to encourage their migrations hither, and raising the conditions of new Appropriations of Lands. — He has obstructed the Administration of Justice, by refusing his Assent to Laws for establishing Judiciary powers. — He has made Judges dependent on his Will alone, for the tenure of their offices, and the amount and payment of their salaries. — He has erected a multitude of New Offices, and sent hither swarms of Officers to harrass our people, and eat out their substance. — He has kept among us, in times of peace, Standing Armies without the Consent of our legislatures. — He has affected to render the Military independent of and superior to the Civil power. — He has combined with others to subject us to a jurisdiction foreign to our constitution, and unacknowledged by our laws; giving his Assent to their Acts of pretended Legislation: — For Quartering large bodies of armed troops among us: — For protecting them, by a mock Trial, from punishment for any Murders which they should commit on the Inhabitants of these States: — For cutting off our Trade with all parts of the world: — For imposing Taxes on us without our Consent: — For depriving us in many cases, of the benefits of Trial by jury: — For transporting us beyond Seas to be tried for pretended offences: — For abolishing the free System of English Laws in a neighbouring Province, establishing therein an Arbitrary government, and enlarging its Boundaries so as to render it at once an example and fit instrument for introducing the same absolute rule into these Colonies: — For taking away our Charters, abolishing our most valuable Laws, and altering fundamentally the Forms of our Governments: — For suspending our own Legislatures, and declaring themselves invested with power to legislate for us in all cases whatsoever. — He has abdicated Government here, by declaring us out of his Protection and waging War against us. — He has plundered our seas, ravaged our Coasts, burnt our towns, and destroyed the lives of our people. — He is at this time transporting large Armies of foreign Mercenaries to compleat the works of death, desolation and tyranny, already begun with circumstances of Cruelty & perfidy scarcely paralleled in the most barbarous ages, and totally unworthy the Head of a civilized nation. — He has constrained our fellow Citizens taken Captive on the high Seas to bear Arms against their Country, to become the executioners of their friends and Brethren, or to fall themselves by their Hands. — He has excited domestic insurrections amongst us, and has endeavoured to bring on the inhabitants of our frontiers, the merciless Indian Savages, whose known rule of warfare, is an undistinguished destruction of all ages, sexes and conditions. In every stage of these Oppressions We have Petitioned for Redress in the most humble terms: Our repeated Petitions have been answered only by repeated injury. A Prince, whose character is thus marked by every act which may define a Tyrant, is unfit to be the ruler of a free people. Nor have We been wanting in attentions to our British brethren. We have warned them from time to time of attempts by their legislature to extend an unwarrantable jurisdiction over us. We have reminded them of the circumstances of our emigration and settlement here. We have appealed to their native justice and magnanimity, and we have conjured them by the ties of our common kindred to disavow these usurpations, which, would inevitably interrupt our connections and correspondence. They too have been deaf to the voice of justice and of consanguinity. We must, therefore, acquiesce in the necessity, which denounces our Separation, and hold them, as we hold the rest of mankind, Enemies in War, in Peace Friends. —

We, therefore, the Representatives of the united States of America, in General Congress, Assembled, appealing to the Supreme Judge of the world for the rectitude of our intentions, do, in the Name, and by Authority of the good People of these Colonies, solemnly publish and declare, That these United Colonies are, and of Right ought to be Free and Independent States; that they are Absolved from all Allegiance to the British Crown, and that all political connection between them and the State of Great Britain, is and ought to be totally dissolved; and that as Free and Independent States, they have full Power to levy War, conclude Peace, contract Alliances, establish Commerce, and to do all other Acts and Things which Independent States may of right do. — And for the support of this Declaration, with a firm reliance on the protection of divine Providence, we mutually pledge to each other our Lives, our Fortunes and our sacred Honor.

John Hancock

Button Gwinnett
Lyman Hall
Geo Walton.

Wm Hooper
Joseph Hewes,
John Penn

Edward Rutledge.

Thos Heyward Junr.
Thomas Lynch Junr.
Arthur Middleton

Samuel Chase
Wm Paca
Thos Stone
Charles Carroll of Carrollton

George Wythe
Richard Henry Lee
Th Jefferson
Benja Harrison
Thos Nelson jr.
Francis Lightfoot Lee
Carter Braxton

Robt Morris
Benjamin Rush
Benja Franklin
John Morton
Geo Clymer
Jas. Smith
Geo. Taylor
James Wilson
Geo. Ross
Caesar Rodney
Geo Read
Tho M:Kean

Wm Floyd
Phil. Livingston
Frans. Lewis
Lewis Morris
Richd Stockton
Jno Witherspoon
Fras. Hopkinson
John Hart
Abra Clark

Josiah Bartlett
Wm Whipple
Saml Adams
John Adams
Robt Treat Paine
Elbridge Gerry
Step Hopkins
William Ellery
Roger Sherman
Saml Huntington
Wm Williams
Oliver Wolcott
Matthew Thornton

3. The First Woman to Serve in the Armed Forces of the United States

This document proves that a woman served in the armed forces of the United States during the Revolutionary War. Deborah Sampson, of Middleboro, Massachusetts, enlisted as a private in the Fourth Massachusetts Regiment under the name of Robert Shurtleff. She fought for two years before anyone discovered that she was a woman. She was wounded by a musket ball in the battle of Tarrytown and recovered. She was with the army when they captured Cornwallis at Yorktown. "Private Shurtleff" was serving as an aide-de-camp to General Patterson when she fell ill with a fever and was taken to a hospital.

When it was discovered that private Shurtleff was a woman, she, Deborah Sampson, was given an honorable discharge. Her fellow soldiers honored her courage and patriotism by allowing her to parade down their ranks as she left the army.

In 1818, being older and in need, she applied to the government for the pension for Revolutionary War soldiers and it was granted. She received $96 a year until her death in 1827.

After her death, her aged husband, Benjamin Gannett, who had never served in the army, requested a continuation of her pension for himself. Congress debated this unusual request. It decided that a woman of such courage and devotion to her country could never have married anyone who was not also patriotic. Her husband was granted her pension.

United States —

Massachusetts District —

Deborah Gannett, of Sharon, in the county of Norfolk, and
District of Massachusetts, a resident and native of the United States, and applicant for a pension from the United States,
under an Act of Congress entitled an Act. to provide for certain persons engaged in the land and naval service of the
United States, in the revolutionary war, maketh oath, That she
served as a private soldier, under the name of Robert Shurtleff, in the war of the revolution, upwards of two years in manner following. viz — Enlisted in April 1781. in the company commanded by Captain George Webb. in the Massachusetts Regiment
commanded then by Colonel Shepherd — and afterwards by Colonel Henry Jackson — and served in said corps, in Massachusetts and
New York — until November 1783 — when she was honorably discharg-
ed in writing. Which discharge is lost. During the time of her service, she was at the capture of Lord Cornwallis — was wounded
at Tarrytown — and now receives a pension from the United
States, which pension she hereby relinquishes — She is in such
reduced circumstances, as to require the aid of her country —
for her support ————   Deborah Gannett

Mass. Dis. Se. Sept. 14. 1818

Sworn to before me
        J M Davis
        Dis. Judge
        Mass. Dist

4. Patrick Henry's Instructions to George Henry Clark 1776

This is an official order written by Patrick Henry concerning a part of the Revolutionary War which we do not often hear about. During the war, Patrick Henry was governor of Virginia. He realized the dangerous position of the thirteen colonies, strung along the Atlantic Ocean from Massachusetts and New Hampshire as far south as Georgia. West of these colonies was a wilderness. In this wilderness, in the Illinois and Ohio River regions, were French and Indian settlements. These had been controlled by the British since England defeated the French in Canada almost twenty years earlier. If the British could persuade the French and Indians to turn against the colonists, the United States would be sandwiched between two enemy forces and forced to fight on two fronts.

Patrick Henry sent the daring young surveyor, George Rogers Clark, in charge of an expedition to capture, peacefully if possible, the French and Indian villages.

This paper gave Clark exact instructions. It instructed him to treat the French and Indians well. Clark was warned that these peoples would judge all of the colonists by the behavior of his troops. The soldiers must be honorable or they would bring anger against their country.

Clark was a fair-minded man and his generous treatment of the French won them so that they took the oath of allegiance to the United States. In return they were promised the privileges and liberties of other Americans; foremost among these, freedom of their own religion.

sions favorable or not so of our Commonwealth & will its Government
which Impressions will be had to remove & will produce lasting
Good in its Effects to your Country; These Considerations will make
you cautious & circumspect. Tho' the Delicacy & difficulty of
your Situation, but I doubt not your Virtue will accomplish the
Arduous Work with Honor to yourself & advantage to the Commonwealth. The Advice & assistance of divers good men will be highly
necessary. For at the Distance of your Country, I cannot be consulted.
General Discretionary powers therefore are given you to act for
the best in all Cases where these Instructions are silent, & the
Law has made no provision.

I desire your particular attention to Mrs. Rocheblave &
her Children, & that you suffer them to want for nothing. let Mr.
Rocheblave's property which was taken be restored to his Lady so far
as it can be done. — You had the Sum of sixty pounds —
sent for her use in case you can't find her husband's effects to
restore.

Prudence requires that provisions be laid in to subsist the
Troops you have & those to be expected to arrive with you Colonel
Bowman has contracted to deliver 35.000 lb. Bear Bacon at Kentucky, But Bread must be had at Illinois. You will provide it if
possible before the arrival of the Troops, or the necessity to buy it
becomes generally known as perhaps Advantages may be taken
by raising the price. Lay up also a good stock of Sound flour &c.

There is a Cargo of Goods at a Spanish post near you
belonging either to the Continent or this State. Rather than let
your Troops be naked, you are to take a supply for them out of
these Goods. But this is not to be done but in Case of absolute
Necessity. Let an exact Account be kept of what is used & let
me be acquainted.

In your Negociations or Treaties with the Indians,
you will be assisted by Mr. Todd. Let the Treaties be confined to
the subject of amity & peace & new species & not to touch
the subject of Lands. You may accept of any services they
offer for expelling the English from Detroit & elsewhere. In
case you find presents to the Savages necessary, make them
sparingly as possible, letting them know our stock of Goods is small
at present, but by means of a free Trade with the French & other
nations we expect plenty of Goods before long.

Lieutenant Colonel Montgomery will convey to you
ten thousand pounds for payment of the Troops & for other
Matters requiring Money. In the Distribution of money you
will be careful to keep exact accounts & from time to time
& take security where else proper. I am Sir
                                        Yr. Hbl. Sv.
                                             P. Henry

5. John Paul Jones' Letter to Gouverneur Morris 1782

We cannot be proud of the way John Paul Jones was treated after his heroism in the War for Independence. Yet notice how courteously he wrote to Gouverneur Morris, although he must have known that Congress had gone back on its promise to him. Jones wrote from New Hampshire, where he had been supervising the construction of the ship *America*, which Congress had promised that Jones should command in return for his services in the war. Before the ship was completed, Congress decided to turn the *America* over to France to replace a ship which that nation had lost at Boston.

John Paul Jones was a British sailor who came to the colonies shortly before the outbreak of the War for Independence. He asked for a place in the United States Navy and became one of its best and bravest naval officers. Commanding second-rate ships, he staged commando raids on the British coast and on British shipping. His bravery and many unexpected victories made him famous.

One of the greatest battles was between his ship, *Bonhomme Richard*, and the British ship, *Serapis*. When the British captain of the much larger ship believed that Jones was defeated and asked if he wanted to surrender, John Paul Jones cried, "I have only begun to fight." He went on to win the battle.

After the War for Independence ended, Congress gave Jones a vote of thanks but they had not paid him a dollar in five years for his services. Congress voted that the United States would not have a navy. Jones no longer had a job. After the ship *America* was promised to him, then denied him, he left this country for Russia, where he was made an admiral. Some years later John Paul Jones died in Paris. After many years, in 1905, his body was returned to America and tribute was paid, at last, to a great naval hero.

9

You know me I find, since you are sure I
will rejoice at the present appearances of
Peace — An honorable Peace is and always
was my first wish. I can take no delight
in the effusion of human Blood. but if this
War should continue I wish to have the
most active part in it. — With the
highest sense of your kind attentions and
good opinion, and with the most earnest
desire to deserve, by my conduct the delicate
Praises of a Friend of your high worth and
Public Spirit, I am, sincerely and affectionately
your most Obliged

6. Treaty of Paris 1783

The full treaty was a booklet twenty-four pages long, written entirely by hand. When General Cornwallis surrendered at York-town, the fighting of the Revolutionary War was over, but it took two more years to bring about England's written recognition of American independence. The reason for this delay was that France was fighting as an ally of America, and Spain had an alliance with France. America had to wait for the final papers of peace until France and Spain could also make a treaty with England. At last the peace was signed in Paris. Benjamin Franklin, John Adams and John Jay signed for the new United States of America. (Notice how many times we find the same men working for the good of their country.)

American independence was officially recognized. The British agreed to remove their troops from American soil, to grant the new nation land west to the Mississippi, and also to grant fishing rights in British North American waters.

without Difficulty and without requiring any Compensation.

Article 10th..

The solemn Ratifications of the present Treaty expedited in good & due Form shall be exchanged between the contracting Parties in the Space of Six Months or sooner if possible to be computed from the Day of the Signature of the present Treaty. In Witness whereof we the undersigned their Ministers Plenipotentiary have in their Name and in Virtue of our Full Powers signed with our Hands the present Definitive Treaty, and caused the Seals of our Arms to be affix'd thereto.

Done at Paris, this third Day of September, In the Year of our Lord one thousand seven hundred & eighty three. —

D Hartley   John Adams:—

B Franklin   John Jay——

7. Washington's Copy of the Constitution 1787

What do you think of when you hear the name of George Washington? Do you think of a great general? The first President of the United States? The father of his country? He was all these, but Washington's help in planning a new form of government was one of his greatest services to his country.

He had suffered great hardship in the war: cold, hunger and strain. He was tired and troubled with rheumatism. His home and farms in Virginia were run down. He needed very badly to manage them again. Washington longed to stay at home and rest and be with his family.

But, now that the war was over, the various states began to disagree. There were no written laws by which all the states were governed. Washington realized that the future of this new nation was in grave danger if the convention which the states were to hold did not form a government that would be fair to all. So he left his home to attend the convention.

During four hot summer months, the members of the convention struggled to write a just set of laws. In this rough draft of the Constitution are corrections written in by Washington himself.

Washington did not write the Constitution. It was worked out thoughtfully, step by step, by the debate and labor of all men who attended the convention. Washington was elected president of the convention. He presided at the meetings where he helped to bring about peaceful settlements when tempers flared. It is said that his influence was so great that if the Constitution had not come out under his name, it would not have been ratified by the states. He gave a fine example of a man's sacrificing his own plans and desires for the good of his country.

WE the People of the States of New-Hampfhire, Maffachufetts, Rhode-Ifland and Providence Plan-tations, Connecticut, New-York, New-Jerfey, Penn-fylvania, Delaware, Maryland, Virginia, North-Caro-lina, South-Carolina, and Georgia, do ordain, declare and eftablifh the following Conftitution for the Govern-ment of Ourfelves and our Pofterity.

ARTICLE I.

The ftile of this Government fhall be, " The United States of America."

II.

The Government fhall confift of fupreme legiflative, executive and judicial powers.

III.

The legiflative power fhall be vefted in a Congrefs, to confift of two feparate and diftinct bodies of men, a Houfe of Reprefentatives, and a Senate; ~~each of which fhall, in all cafes, have a negative on the other. The Legiflature fhall meet on the firft Monday in December in every year.~~

[left margin handwritten: The Legiflature fhall meet at leaft once in every year, and that meeting fhall be on the firft Monday in December unlefs a different day fhall be appointed by law.]

IV.

Sect. 1. The Members of the Houfe of Reprefentatives fhall be chofen eve-ry fecond year, by the people of the feveral States comprehended within this Union. The qualifications of the electors fhall be the fame, from time to time, as thofe of the electors in the feveral States, of the moft numerous branch of their own legiflatures.

Sect. 2. Every Member of the Houfe of Reprefentatives fhall be of the age of twenty-five years at leaft; fhall have been a citizen of the United States for at leaft ____ years before his election; and fhall be, at the time of his e-lection, ____ of the State in which he fhall be chofen

Sect. 3. The Houfe of Reprefentatives fhall, at its firft formation, and until the number of citizens and inhabitants fhall be taken in the manner herein af-ter defcribed, confift of fixty-five Members, of whom three fhall be chofen in New-Hampfhire, eight in Maffachufetts, one in Rhode-Ifland and Providence Plantations, five in Connecticut, fix in New-York, four in New-Jerfey, eight in Pennfylvania, one in Delaware, fix in Maryland, ten in Virginia, five in North-Carolina, five in South-Carolina, and three in Georgia.

Sect. 4. As the proportions of numbers in the different States will alter from time to time; as fome of the States may hereafter be divided; as others may be enlarged by addition of territory; as two or more States may be united; as new States will be erected within the limits of the United States, the Legifla-ture fhall, in each of thefe cafes, regulate the number of reprefentatives by the number of inhabitants, according to the ____ rate of one for every forty thoufand. *Provided that every State fhall have at leaft one reprefentative.*

Sect. 5. All bills for raifing or appropriating money, and for fixing the fala-ries of the officers of government, fhall originate in the Houfe of Reprefenta-tives, and fhall not be altered or amended by the Senate. No money fhall be drawn from the public Treafury, but in purfuance of appropriations that fhall originate in the Houfe of Reprefentatives.

[left margin handwritten: ftruck out]

Sect. 6. The Houfe of Reprefentatives fhall have the fole power of impeach-ment. It fhall choofe its Speaker and other officers.

Sect. 7. Vacancies in the Houfe of Reprefentatives fhall be fupplied by writs of election from the executive authority of the State, in the reprefentation from which they fhall happen. V.

8. The Northwest Ordinance 1787

In the Treaty of Paris, England granted the new nation of America all the land west of the states to the Mississippi River. This was a vast tract of wilderness, much too large and with too few people to be a state. Yet there were settlements here, among them the French villages which Clark won over during the Revolution. There were also Detroit and other fur-trading centers. The people who lived in this great tract of land needed to be recognized in the new government. A committee was named to draw up a set of laws (an ordinance) which would state the rights of the people living in the territory northwest of the Ohio River.

This agreement, between the thirteen original states and the people of the territory, promised religious liberty, the right of habeas corpus, trial by jury. It forbade slavery and encouraged public education. It provided that, when enough people lived in a certain area, these people could petition to become a state. The state would be accepted into the United States with the full rights of the original states.

This ordinance proved that the new nation intended to treat fairly the settlers on its public lands. Such fairness helped the United States to grow rapidly in the west. From the Northwest Territory, the following states were later formed and joined the union: Ohio 1803, Indiana 1816, Illinois 1818, Michigan 1837, Wisconsin 1848.

An ORDINANCE for the GOVERNMENT of the TERRITORY of the UNITED STATES, North-Weſt of the RIVER OHIO.

BE IT ORDAINED by the United States in Congreſs aſſembled, That the ſaid territory, for the purpoſes of temporary government, be one diſtrict; ſubject, however, to be divided into two diſtricts, as future circumſtances may, in the opinion of Congreſs, make it expedient.

Be it ordained by the authority aforeſaid, That the eſtates both of reſident and non-reſident proprietors in the ſaid territory, dying inteſtate, ſhall deſcend to, and be diſtributed among their children, and the deſcendants of a deceaſed child in equal parts; the deſcendants of a deceaſed child or grand-child, to take the ſhare of their deceaſed parent in equal parts among them: And where there ſhall be no children or deſcendants, then in equal parts to the next of kin, in equal degree; and among collaterals, the children of a deceaſed brother or ſiſter of the inteſtate, ſhall have in equal parts among them their deceaſed parents ſhare; and there ſhall in no caſe be a diſtinction between kindred of the whole and half blood; ſaving in all caſes to the widow of the inteſtate, her third part of the real eſtate for life, and one third part of the perſonal eſtate; and this law relative to deſcents and dower, ſhall remain in full force until altered by the legiſlature of the diſtrict. ———— And until the governor and judges ſhall adopt laws as herein after mentioned, eſtates in the ſaid territory may be deviſed or bequeathed by wills in writing, ſigned and ſealed by him or her, in whom the eſtate may be, (being of full age) and atteſted by three witneſſes; — and real eſtates may be conveyed by leaſe and releaſe, or bargain and ſale, ſigned, ſealed, and delivered by the perſon being of full age, in whom the eſtate may be, and atteſted by two witneſſes, provided ſuch wills be duly proved, and ſuch conveyances be acknowledged, or the execution thereof duly proved, and be recorded within one year after proper magiſtrates, courts, and regiſters ſhall be appointed for that purpoſe; and perſonal property may be transferred by delivery, ſaving, however, to the French and Canadian inhabitants, and other ſettlers of the Kaſkaſkies, Saint Vincent's, and the neighbouring villages, who have heretofore profeſſed themſelves citizens of Virginia, their laws and cuſtoms now in force among them, relative to the deſcent and conveyance of property.

Be it ordained by the authority aforeſaid, That there ſhall be appointed from time to time, by Congreſs, a governor, whoſe commiſſion ſhall continue in force for the term of three years, unleſs ſooner revoked by Congreſs; he ſhall reſide in the diſtrict, and have a freehold eſtate therein, in one thouſand acres of land, while in the exerciſe of his office.

There ſhall be appointed from time to time, by Congreſs, a ſecretary, whoſe commiſſion ſhall continue in force for four years, unleſs ſooner revoked, he ſhall reſide in the diſtrict, and have a freehold eſtate therein, in five hundred acres of land, while in the exerciſe of his office; it ſhall be his duty to keep and preſerve the acts and laws paſſed by the legiſlature, and the public records of the diſtrict, and the proceedings of the governor in his executive department; and tranſmit authentic copies of ſuch acts and proceedings, every ſix months, to the ſecretary of Congreſs: There ſhall alſo be appointed a court to conſiſt of three judges, any two of whom to form a court, who ſhall have a common law juriſdiction, and reſide in the diſtrict, and have each therein a freehold eſtate in five hundred acres of land, while in the exerciſe of their offices; and their commiſſions ſhall continue in force during good behaviour.

The governor and judges, or a majority of them, ſhall adopt and publiſh in the diſtrict, ſuch laws of the original ſtates, criminal and civil, as may be neceſſary, and beſt ſuited to the circumſtances of the diſtrict, and report them to Congreſs, from time to time, which laws ſhall be in force in the diſtrict until the organization of the general aſſembly therein, unleſs diſapproved of by Congreſs; but afterwards the legiſlature ſhall have authority to alter them as they ſhall think fit.

The governor for the time being, ſhall be commander in chief of the militia, appoint and commiſſion all officers in the ſame, below the rank of general officers; all general officers ſhall be appointed and commiſſioned by Congreſs.

Previous to the organization of the general aſſembly, the governor ſhall appoint ſuch magiſtrates and other civil officers, in each county or townſhip, as he ſhall find neceſſary for the preſervation of the peace and good order in the ſame: After the general aſſembly ſhall be organized, the powers and duties of magiſtrates and other civil officers ſhall be regulated and defined by the ſaid aſſembly; but all magiſtrates and other civil officers, not herein otherwiſe directed, ſhall, during the continuance of this temporary government, be appointed by the governor.

For the prevention of crimes and injuries, the laws to be adopted or made ſhall have force in all parts of the diſtrict, and for the execution of proceſs, criminal and civil, the governor ſhall make proper diviſions thereof——and he ſhall proceed from time to time, as circumſtances may require, to lay out the parts of the diſtrict in which the Indian titles ſhall have been extinguiſhed, into counties and townſhips, ſubject, however, to ſuch alterations as may thereafter be made by the legiſlature.

So ſoon as there ſhall be five thouſand free male inhabitants, of full age, in the diſtrict, upon giving proof thereof to the governor, they ſhall receive authority, with time and place, to elect repreſentatives from their counties or townſhips, to repreſent them in the general aſſembly; provided that for every five hundred free male inhabitants there ſhall be one repreſentative, and ſo on progreſſively with the number of free male inhabitants, ſhall the right of repreſentation increaſe, until the number of repreſentatives ſhall amount to twenty-five, after which the number and proportion of repreſentatives ſhall be regulated by the legiſlature; provided that no perſon be eligible or qualified to act as a repreſentative, unleſs he ſhall have been a citizen of one of the United States three years and be a reſident in the diſtrict, or unleſs he ſhall have reſided in the diſtrict three years, and in either caſe ſhall likewiſe hold in his own right, in fee ſimple, two hundred acres of land within the ſame:——Provided alſo, that a freehold in fifty acres of land in the diſtrict, having been a citizen of one of the ſtates, and being reſident in the diſtrict; or the like freehold and two years reſidence in the diſtrict ſhall be neceſſary to qualify a man as an elector of a repreſentative.

The repreſentatives thus elected, ſhall ſerve for the term of two years, and in caſe of the death of a repreſentative, or removal from office, the governor ſhall iſſue a writ to the county or townſhip for which he was a member, to elect another in his ſtead, to ſerve for the reſidue of the term.

The general aſſembly, or legiſlature, ſhall conſiſt of the governor, legiſlative council, and a houſe of repreſentatives. The legiſlative council ſhall conſiſt of five members, to continue in office five years, unleſs ſooner removed by Congreſs, any three of whom to be a quorum, and the members of the council ſhall be nominated and appointed in the following manner, to wit: As ſoon as repreſentatives ſhall be elected, the governor ſhall appoint a time and place for them to meet together, and, when met, they ſhall nominate ten perſons, reſidents in the diſtrict, and each poſſeſſed of a freehold in five hundred acres of land, and return their names to Congreſs; five of whom Congreſs ſhall appoint and commiſſion to ſerve as aforeſaid; and whenever a vacancy ſhall happen in the council, by death or removal from office, the houſe of repreſentatives ſhall nominate two perſons, qualified as aforeſaid, for each vacancy, and return their names to Congreſs; one of whom Congreſs ſhall appoint and commiſſion for the reſidue of the term; and every five years, four months at leaſt before the expiration of the time of ſervice of the members of council, the ſaid houſe ſhall nominate ten perſons, qualified as aforeſaid, and return their names to Congreſs, five of whom Congreſs ſhall appoint and commiſſion to ſerve as members of the council five years, unleſs ſooner removed. And the governor, legiſlative council, and houſe of re-

9.   The Bill of Rights 1789-1791

The ink and writing on the Bill of Rights are faded with age, but every freedom that it promised belongs to you and me today. Do you know how precious these freedoms are? Do you realize how many people, living in the world right now, do not enjoy these freedoms and long for them?

The men who wrote our Constitution believed they had formed a good set of laws to govern our nation. But, these same men said, there are certain natural rights which belong to every human being and no government should take these natural rights from a man. So they added to the Constitution a bill of ten rights.

Among the most precious of these rights is FREEDOM OF RELIGION. We can thank a man who lived a hundred and fifty years before the Bill of Rights was written for fighting for religious freedom in the New World. Roger Williams, a young English minister, formed the settlement of Providence, R. I., in 1636, and declared that every individual had a right to his own religious belief, whether it was pagan, Jewish, Catholic or Protestant.

FREEDOM OF SPEECH guarantees our right to talk openly about our ideas without fear of punishment.

FREEDOM OF THE PRESS means that newspapers, magazines and books may print all sides of an argument—so that we can be informed and make up our minds what is right.

Read all the other "rights" guaranteed to you. Use your "freedom of speech" to discuss these with others. Notice the signature at the bottom of the bill. This is the same John Adams who signed other American documents. He is one of the men who lived long ago and left gifts of freedom to us which we should treasure and give thanks for.

Congress OF THE United States,

begun and held at the City of New York, on
Wednesday, the fourth of March, one thousand seven hundred and eighty nine.

THE Conventions of a number of the States having, at the time of their adopting the Constitution, expressed a desire, in order to prevent misconstruction or abuse of its powers, that further declaratory and restrictive clauses should be added: And as extending the ground of public confidence in the Government, will best ensure the beneficent ends of its institution.

RESOLVED, by the Senate and House of Representatives of the United States of America in Congress assembled, two thirds of both Houses concurring, That the following Articles be proposed to the Legislatures of the several States, as Amendments to the Constitution of the United States, all, or any of which Articles, when ratified by three fourths of the said Legislatures, to be valid to all intents and purposes, as part of the said Constitution; viz.

ARTICLES in addition to, and Amendment of the Constitution of the United States of America, proposed by Congress, and ratified by the Legislatures of the several States, pursuant to the fifth Article of the original Constitution.

Article the first ... After the first enumeration required by the first Article of the Constitution, there shall be one Representative for every thirty thousand, until the number shall amount to one hundred, after which, the proportion shall be so regulated by Congress, that there shall be not less than one hundred Representatives, nor less than one Representative for every forty thousand persons, until the number of Representatives shall amount to two hundred, after which the proportion shall be so regulated by Congress, that there shall not be less than two hundred Representatives, nor more than one Representative for every fifty thousand persons.

Article the second ... No law, varying the compensation for the services of the Senators and Representatives, shall take effect, until an election of Representatives shall have intervened.

Article the third ... Congress shall make no law respecting an establishment of religion, or prohibiting the free exercise thereof; or abridging the freedom of speech, or of the press; or the right of the people peaceably to assemble, and to petition the Government for a redress of grievances.

Article the fourth ... A well regulated Militia, being necessary to the security of a free State, the right of the people to keep and bear Arms, shall not be infringed.

Article the fifth ... No Soldier shall, in time of peace, be quartered in any house, without the consent of the owner, nor in time of war, but in a manner to be prescribed by law.

Article the sixth ... The right of the people to be secure in their persons, houses, papers, and effects, against unreasonable searches and seizures, shall not be violated, and no Warrants shall issue, but upon probable cause, supported by oath or affirmation, and particularly describing the place to be searched, and the persons or things to be seized.

Article the seventh ... No person shall be held to answer for a capital, or otherwise infamous crime, unless on a presentment or indictment of a grand jury, except in cases arising in the land or naval forces, or in the Militia, when in actual service in time of War or public danger; nor shall any person be subject for the same offence to be twice put in jeopardy of life or limb; nor shall be compelled in any criminal case, to be a witness against himself, nor be deprived of life, liberty, or property, without due process of law; nor shall private property be taken for public use, without just compensation.

Article the eighth ... In all criminal prosecutions, the accused shall enjoy the right to a speedy and public trial, by an impartial jury of the State and district wherein the crime shall have been committed, which district shall have been previously ascertained by law, and to be informed of the nature and cause of the accusation; to be confronted with the witnesses against him; to have compulsory process for obtaining witnesses in his favor, and to have the assistance of counsel for his defence.

Article the ninth ... In suits at common law, where the value in controversy shall exceed twenty dollars, the right of trial by jury shall be preserved, and no fact tried by a jury, shall be otherwise re-examined in any Court of the United States, than according to the rules of the common law.

Article the tenth ... Excessive bail shall not be required, nor excessive fines imposed, nor cruel and unusual punishments inflicted.

Article the eleventh ... The enumeration in the Constitution, of certain rights, shall not be construed to deny or disparage others retained by the people.

Article the twelfth ... The powers not delegated to the United States by the Constitution, nor prohibited by it to the States, are reserved to the States respectively, or to the people.

Frederick Augustus Muhlenberg, Speaker of the House of Representatives.

John Adams, Vice President of the United States, and President of the Senate.

ATTEST,

John Beckley, Clerk of the House of Representatives.

Sam. A. Otis Secretary of the Senate.

10.   Washington's Last Official Letter 1796

Washington was weary and ill after the Revolutionary War. He wanted to remain at home, but he knew his country needed him. He helped form the Constitution, then became President of the United States. After his first term, again he wished to go home, but the country was still young and inexperienced. It needed help so much that Washington agreed to serve another term. However, in 1796, he said he had given most of his life to the service of his country. He was in his sixties and he wanted rest. Since he loved his country deeply, he did not wish to leave office without a final letter of advice and farewell.

Washington's farewell letter was written only after great thought and after seeking advice from other wise and thoughtful men. Alexander Hamilton and James Madison helped Washington prepare this letter, but it is entirely in Washington's handwriting. He caused it to be published in a newspaper, the *American Daily Advertiser*, so that every person could read it.

Washington warned against jealousy among the different parts of the country. He knew that if one section tried to seek its own gain without thought for the rights of the others, quarreling and hatred could destroy the nation.

He believed that America had a well-planned system of government, and any officials who followed the laws could give the people good government.

He believed that the young nation of America should stay out of the affairs of all other nations. It should try to become strong and pay no attention to the strife which might go on in other parts of the world.

Think of what the world was like when Washington gave this advice. Do you think he would give the same advice if he lived today? What differences in the world might change his opinion today?

Friends and Fellow Citizens

The quotation ~~which you will~~ find in this ~~following~~ address, was composed, and intended to have been published in the year 1792; in time to have appeared to the Electors of the President & Vice President of the United States, the determination of the former previous ~~as to their~~ Election ~~thereon expressed before the Election~~ ~~could then be~~ ~~be made:~~ but the solicitude ~~of~~ my confidential ~~friends~~ pressed, ~~whose approbation~~ ~~fixes~~ ~~intention, and~~ ~~whose judgment I discover much rely~~ ~~(particularly in one who was privy to the~~ ~~attempt)~~ that I would suspend ~~my deter~~ ~~mination,~~ added to the peculiar situation of our foreign affairs at that epoch, in ~~pro~~ du:

ced

————————

* Mr Madison

(19)

been blessed amidst the tumults which have harrassed other countries. ~~and~~ ~~involved~~ in all the horrors of War — I leave you with undefiled hands — an uncorrupted heart — and with ardent vows to heaven for the Wel-fare & happiness of that country in which I and my forefathers to the third or fourth Progenitor drew our first breath. —

G:º Washington

11. Log of the U. S. Frigate Constitution (Old Ironsides) 1812-1815

The log of the U.S. Frigate *Constitution* tells of her victorious battles at sea against British ships. The War of 1812 was mainly a naval war. Following the War for Independence, the United States sold every ship in its navy. Then England and other European countries, as well as the Barbary pirates, took advantage of the naval weakness of the new nation. They stole valuable cargo from United States merchant ships. They forced American sailors onto British ships to work when they were short of men. At last Congress decided to build six frigates to protect the rights of the United States at sea. One of these frigates was the *Constitution.* Her heavy oak beams were joined together with copper fittings and bolts made by the coppersmith Paul Revere.

In her battle with the English ship *Guerrière*, a heavy shot hit the strong oak side of the *Constitution* and bounded off it into the water. The sailors cried that her sides must be made of iron, so she came to be called *Old Ironsides.*

The *Constitution* was at sea when the peace was signed which ended the War of 1812. Her log shows that her captain, Isaac Hull, did not hear of the peace for some time. She fought and captured several ships after the war was over. One of the enemy ships boarded had recently left port. Its crew told Captain Hull that the war was at an end.

When *Old Ironsides* was old and unfit for service, she was to be destroyed. Oliver Wendell Holmes wrote a poem about her which stirred the nation.

> Ay, tear her tattered ensign down!
> Long has it waved on high
> And many an eye has danced to see
> That banner in the sky.

Demands poured in to the navy to save *Old Ironsides.* Public contributions from people all over the country paid to have her restored. Today, *Old Ironsides* is berthed in Boston Naval Harbor, where you may go to see her.

Remarks and Occurrences on board U. S. frigate Constitution Charles Stewart Esq. Commr. on a Cruise

Wednesday February 8. 1815.

H.	K.	F.	Courses.	Winds	Lee way
1	8	—	East	S. W.	
2	8				
3	8				
4	8				
5	7				
6	7	4			
7	10				
8	9				
9	lying to		Alp S. by E.		
10			Off S.E. by E.		
11					
12					
1					
2					
3	lying to		Alp S. by E.		
4			Off S. E.		
5					
6					
7	2	4	N. by E		
8	8	—	E. by S.		
9	2	—	E. by N.		
10	5	—			
11	4				
12	2	4	East		

First part fresh breezes with squalls and cloudy.

Middle part like weather.

Latter part baffling variable winds. At 7h. 30m. A. M. spoke and boarded the barque Julia under Hamburg colours from Cork bound to Lisbon out 15 days, informed us that the news at Cork when they left was, that peace had been signed at Ghent between the British and American Commissioners. At meridian discovered a sail on the larboard bow, hauled up and made sail in chase.

	Course	Distance	Departure	Diff. Lat.	Lat. by Act.	Lat. Obsd.	Long. in	Longde. by Chronometer	Longde. by Observation	Variation	Wounded	Killed	Sick	Died
				5. 30. N.		42 26 N.								

12. The Star-Spangled Banner 1814

Everyone knows that "The Star-Spangled Banner" is America's national anthem. It was written during a battle of the War of 1812.

A fleet of British ships was drawn up at the entrance of Baltimore Harbor to capture Fort McHenry and take the city of Baltimore. Francis Scott Key was a lawyer who went out to the British ships under a flag of truce. His business was to ask for the release of an American citizen whom the British were holding as hostage. While Key was on the British ship, the fleet began a twenty-five-hour bombardment of Fort McHenry. Key was under guard and had to watch the shelling of his own fort and city. All night he watched anxiously but could not tell whether or not the fort was being forced to surrender. Then morning came. "By the dawn's early light" he saw "the broad stripes and bright stars" still waving above the fort. Key was so proud and thankful that he wrote a poem on the back of a letter which he had in his pocket.

When he was allowed to returned to shore, he wrote the copy you see here. He formed the words to fit a tune which was popular at that time. He showed the song to his brother-in-law, Judge Nicholson, who took it to a printer. The printer published hand-bills of the song and newspapers reprinted it. Everywhere people began to sing it because the song put into words the things which all Americans felt in their hearts about the flag and their country.

O say can you see, ~~through~~ by the dawn's early light,
What so proudly we hail'd at the twilight's last gleaming,
Whose broad stripes & bright stars through the perilous fight
O'er the ramparts we watch'd, were so gallantly streaming?
    And the rocket's red glare, the bomb bursting in air,
    Gave proof through the night that our flag was still there,
O say does that star-spangled banner yet wave
    O'er the land of the free & the home of the brave?

On the shore dimly seen through the mists of the deep,
    Where the foe's haughty host in dread silence reposes,
What is that which the breeze, o'er the towering steep,
    As it fitfully blows, half conceals, half discloses?
    Now it catches the gleam of the morning's first beam,
    In full glory reflected now shines in the stream,
'Tis the star-spangled banner — O long may it wave
    O'er the land of the free & the home of the brave!

And where is that band who so vauntingly swore,
    That the havoc of war & the battle's confusion
A home & a Country should leave us no more?
— ~~Their~~
    Their blood has wash'd out their foul footstep's pollution.
No refuge could save the hireling & slave
From the terror of flight or the gloom of the grave,
And the star-spangled banner in triumph doth wave
    O'er the land of the free & the home of the brave.

O thus be it ever when freemen shall stand
    Between their lov'd home & the war's desolation!
Blest with vict'ry & peace may the heav'n rescued land
Praise the power that hath made & preserv'd us a nation!
    Then conquer we must, when our cause it is just,
    And this be our motto — "In God is our trust,"
And the star-spangled banner in triumph shall wave
    O'er the land of the free & the home of the brave. —

24

13. Jackson's Letter Describing the Battle of New Orleans 1815

The War of 1812 was primarily a naval war, but one land battle proved important for several reasons. The battle of New Orleans is described here by General Andrew Jackson, who wrote from camp. The last paragraphs of this letter show the quick mind and courage of Jackson in taking advantage of a mistake made by a British officer. After a day of battle in which Jackson had almost won, then found himself suddenly routed and in a dangerous position, a truce was called. The commanders of both sides agreed that there would be no more fighting until twelve o'clock of that day. The British officer and his troops, who had managed to cross the river and entrench themselves on Jackson's side, recrossed the river during the truce to consult with other British troops. Jackson had promised "no fighting and no re-enforcements to be brought up" but he had *not* promised that he would not *move* his troops. Eagerly and swiftly he brought up his ranks to re-occupy the important position he had lost to the British the day before.

It was this resourcefulness that gained "Old Hickory," as Jackson was called, the popularity that later made him President of the United States.

His victory also stopped the muttering of many of the states against the poor conduct of the war. Their threats of disunion ceased.

The battle of New Orleans was won against a superior British fleet and army because different groups of people in the United States, who had been unfriendly, joined together when they saw their loved country threatened. Jackson's forces were made up of his own Tennessee frontiersmen and a Kentucky regiment. These tough men had never got along with the aristocratic French and Creole settlers of Louisiana, yet the French fought with Jackson when the moment of battle came. Black freedmen from the island of Santo Domingo fought with him, too. Perhaps most surprising, Jean Laffitte and his pirate crew, all with a price on their heads, risked prison to fight with Jackson for America, which they called their country, too.

Camp 4 miles below Orleans

Sir   9th Jan: 1815.

During the days of the 6th & 7th the enemy had been
actively employed in making preparations for an attack on my lines. With
infinite labour they had succeeded on the night of the 7th in getting their boats
across from the lake to the river, by widening & deepening the canal so while
they had affected their disembarkation. It had not been in my power to im-
=pede these operations by a general attack; Added to other reasons the nature of
the troops under my command mostly militia, rendered it too hazardous to attempt
extensive offensive movements in an open country, against a numerous &
well disciplined army. Altho my forces, as a number, had been increased
by the arrival of the Kentucky division my strength had received
very little addition; a small portion only of that detachment being provided with arms. Compelled thus to wait the attack
of the enemy I took every measure to repel it when made it & to defeat
the object he had in view. Genl. Morgan with the Orleans contingent
the Louisiana militia & a strong detachment of the Kentucky troops occupied
an entrenched Camp on the opposite side of the river, protected by strong bat-
=teries on the bank, erected & superintended by Commodore Patterson.

In my encampment every thing was ready for action when early on the
morning of the 8th the enemy after throwing a heavy shower of bombs &
Congreve rockets advanced their columns on my right & left to storm my
entrenchments. I cannot speak sufficiently in praise of the firmness
& deliberation with which my whole line received their approach:— more
could not have been expected from veterans inured to war. From the
hour the fire of the small arms was as incessant & severe as can be imagined.
The artillery too, directed by officers who displayed equal skill & courage
did great execution. Yet the columns of the enemy continued to advance
with a firmness which reflects upon them the greatest credit. Twice the
Column which approached me on my left was repulsed by the troops of Genl.
Carroll — those of Genl. Coffee, & a division of the Kentucky militia; &
twice they formed again & renewed the assault. At length however cut
to pieces, they fled in confusion from the field, leaving it covered with their
dead & wounded. The loss which the enemy sustained on this occasion cannot
be estimated at less than 1500 in killed wounded & prisoners. Upwards
of three hundred have already been delivered over for burial; &
my men are still engaged in picking them up within my lines &
carrying them to the point where the enemy are to receive them. This
in addition to the dead & wounded whom the enemy have been enabled to carry
from the field during & since the action & to those who have since died of
the wounds they received. We have taken about 500 prisoners, upwards

The enemy having concentred his forces may
again attempt to drive me from my position by storm
Whenever he does, I have no doubt my men will act
with their usual firmness, & sustain a character now
become dear to them.

                                        I have the honor to be
                                        with great respect
                                        Yr. obt St
                                        Andrew Jackson
                                        Major Genl comdg

14. The Monroe Doctrine 1823

James Monroe and Thomas Jefferson were good friends. Both men were from Virginia. Both loved the United States and served their country in various offices most of their lives. When Jefferson was minister to France, he wrote Monroe a letter (1785) stating his opinion of the conditions in the Old World. At the end of the letter he said he wished Monroe could visit Europe.

Jefferson wrote: "It will make you adore your own country, its soil, its climate, its equality, liberty, laws, people and manners. My God! how little do my countrymen know what precious blessings they are in possession of, and which no other people on earth enjoy. I confess I had no idea myself."

Years later Monroe did go to France as minister from the United States. When he returned, he was elected governor of Virginia. After that he was sent to France to make the Louisiana Purchase. He was minister to Great Britain, and returned to become Secretary of War during the War of 1812.

When Monroe finally became President of the United States, he often thought about the entanglements of the Old World and how much he wanted to keep America free of Europe's troubles. He discussed the subject with others and formed the Monroe Doctrine, which states clearly the policy of the United States.

The doctrine was a "hands-off" warning to all foreign powers who might have an eye on the new Americas. Briefly it made it clear that the United States would not tolerate interference or attack by a European power upon any North or South American country. A war upon any of these neighbors would be regarded as a war upon the United States.

-ceeds from that, which exists in their respective Governments; and to the defence of our own, which has been achieved by the loss of so much blood and treasure, and matured by the wisdom of their most enlightened Citizens, and under which we have enjoyed unexampled felicity, this whole nation is devoted. We owe it therefore to candor, and to the amicable relations existing between the United States and those powers, to declare that we should consider any attempt on their part to extend their system to any portion of this Hemisphere, as dangerous to our peace and safety. With the existing Colonies or dependencies of any European power, we have not interfered, and shall not interfere. But with the Governments who have declared their Independence, and maintained it, and whose Independence we have, on great consideration, and on just principles, acknowledged, we could not view any interposition for the purpose of oppressing them, or controuling in any other manner, their destiny, by any European power, in any other light, than as the manifestation of an unfriendly disposition towards the United States. In the war between those new Governments and Spain, we declared our neutrality, at the time of their recognition, and to this we have adhered, and shall continue to adhere, provided no change shall occur, which in the judgement of the competent authorities of this Government shall make a corresponding change, on the part of

make a corresponding change, on the part of the United States, indispensable to their security.

The late events in Spain and Portugal, show that Europe is still unsettled. Of this important fact, no stronger proof can be adduced, than that the allied powers should have thought it proper, on any principle satisfactory to themselves, to have interposed by force, in the internal concerns of Spain. To what extent such interposition may be carried, on the same principle, is a question, in which all Independent powers, whose Governments differ from theirs, are interested, even those most remote, and surely none more so than the United States. Our policy in regard to Europe, which was adopted at an early stage of the wars which have so long agitated that quarter of the Globe, nevertheless remains the same, which is, not to interfere in the internal concerns of any of its powers; to consider the Government de facto, as the legitimate for us; to cultivate friendly relations with it, and to preserve those relations by a frank, firm and manly policy, meeting in all instances, the just claims of every power; submitting to injuries from none. But, in regard to those continents, circumstances are eminently and conspicuously different. It is

15. Emancipation Proclamation 1863

The Civil War was the most heartbreaking ever fought by the United States. In every other case, we fought against an outside enemy. In the Civil War, we fought among ourselves, the North against the South. It was a war for ideas and beliefs so that, sometimes, even families were divided. A brother or a father might fight for the South, another brother or son for the North. The family of President Lincoln's Southern wife fought against the union which her husband upheld.

The Civil War was a fight to save the Union of the United States. The South broke away from the North because of the South's strong feeling that state rights should be above federal rights. One of these differences of opinion was over the right to hold slaves.

President Abraham Lincoln did not believe in slavery, but he did not declare war to free the slaves. The war was fought because the South left the Union and Lincoln believed, with all his heart, that the new nation could not survive unless it remained one nation, indivisible. Foreign powers would again try to take this country unless the states were a strong union.

Lincoln believed in a slow *voluntary* freeing of the slaves by each slave state. He formed a plan by which the Federal Government would *pay* each state the value of its slaves when that state abolished slavery. His plan seemed fair, with great respect for each state's rights. But the war made everyone so angry that few people on either side listened to reason.

At last Lincoln decided to make a proclamation that all slaves would be free *without payment* in any state which *was still at war with the Union* on January first, one hundred days later. Lincoln hoped that this threat would bring back into the Union many Southern states—who could then follow the original plan of voluntary freeing of slaves. The anger, revenge and grief of war were so great that no Southern state believed the President was earnestly trying to deal fairly with them. Not one state returned to the Union. Thus the proclamation became law on January first by presidential decree.

By the President of the United States of America:

A Proclamation.

Whereas, on the twenty-second day of September, in the year of our Lord one thousand eight hundred and sixty-two, a proclamation was issued by the President of the United States, containing, among other things, the following, to wit:

"That on the first day of January, in the "year of our Lord one thousand eight hundred "and sixty-three, all persons held as slaves within "any State or designated part of a State, the people "whereof shall then be in rebellion against the "United States, shall be then, thenceforward, and "forever free; and the Executive Government of the "United States, including the military and naval "authority thereof, will recognize and maintain "the freedom of such persons, and will do no act "or acts to repress such persons, or any of them, "in any efforts they may make for their actual "freedom.

"That the Executive will, on the first day

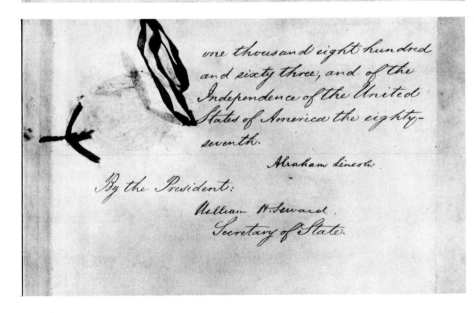

one thousand eight hundred and sixty three, and of the Independence of the United States of America the eighty-seventh.

Abraham Lincoln

By the President:

William H. Seward,
Secretary of State.

16.   Lincoln's Gettysburg Address 1863

The Gettysburg Address can be read in almost any book of great American literature, for the world now recognizes the beauty and inspiration of its words. But in 1863, the committee in charge of the dedication ceremonies at Gettysburg was worried about the kind of speech the President might give!

Eighteen states, led by Pennsylvania, decided to turn the battle-field of Gettysburg into a cemetery. Here they buried the many soldier dead from both North and South and planned to give honor to them all. The committee members agreed to ask the greatest orator in the country, Edward Everett, to make the dedication speech. They sent out printed invitations to all the officials of the country. One went to President Lincoln although the committee expected him to be too busy to attend the ceremony.

When Lincoln accepted, the committee was in a turmoil. President Lincoln was known to enjoy jokes. What if he spoiled the dignity of their ceremony with some of his humor? However, he *was* the President and politeness demanded that Lincoln be asked to say "a few words."

Lincoln felt a deep sympathy for the grief of both North and South in that bitter war. During busy days he prepared his brief talk in his mind. He wrote a rough draft of it before he took the train for Gettysburg. In Gettysburg, on the morning of the dedication, Lincoln revised his rough draft and wrote down the copy which you see here. He held it in his hand as he stood on the platform at the battlefield. When he came to the last lines of his speech, he added two words which he had not written into the copy. They are "under God."

"That this nation, *under God*, shall have a new birth of freedom—and that government of the people, by the people, for the people, shall not perish from this earth."

Four score and seven years ago our fathers
brought forth, upon this continent, a new nation, conceived in Liberty, and dedicated to the proposition
that all men are created equal.

Now we are engaged in a great civil war, test-
ing whether that nation, or any nation, so conceived,
and so dedicated, can long endure. We are met
here on a great battlefield of that war. We have
come
~~met~~ to dedicate a portion of it as a final rest-
for
ing place of those who here gave their lives that
that nation might live. It is altogether fitting
and proper that we should do this.

But in a larger sense we can not dedicate—
we can not consecrate— we can not hallow this
ground. The brave men, living and dead, who strug-
poor
gled here, have consecrated it far above our power
to add or detract. The world will little note,
nor long remember, what we say here, but
can never forget what they did here. It is
for us, the living, rather to be dedicated
work
here to the unfinished which they have,
thus far, so nobly carried on. It is rather

for us to be here dedicated to the great
us
task remaining before— that from these
honored dead we take increased devotion
that
to the cause for which they here gave ~~ga~~
the last full measure of devotion— that
we here highly resolve that these dead
shall not have died in vain; that this
nation shall have a new birth of freedom,
and that this government of the people, by
the people, for the people, shall not perish
from the earth.

17.   The Thirteenth Amendment (Slavery) 1865

The Emancipation Proclamation was a war measure to try to force the South back into the Union. When no Southern state returned, all the slaves in the states which were fighting the Union were set free without payment. But slavery was still legal in all the slave-holding border states which remained in the Union.

As the Civil War drew nearer to an end, the American people grew more and more concerned about slavery. People began to say that now the slaves were free in the South, they should be free in all the nation.

In January 1864, the Senate proposed a resolution to amend the Constitution and remove slavery from the entire country forever. A long and bitter fight in Congress followed. Finally the Thirteenth Amendment was sent to the states for ratification. By law, three-fourths of the states must ratify the amendment before it could be passed. After General Lee surrendered, the North was able to force the defeated Southern states to ratify the amendment as a part of the peace terms. This ended slavery in the United States of America.

IN THE SENATE OF THE UNITED STATES.

January 11. 1864.

Mr. Henderson asked and, by unanimous consent, obtained leave to bring in the following ~~bill~~ *Joint Resolution* ; which was read twice and referred to the Committee on the Judiciary.

February 10. 1864.

Reported by Mr. Trumbull with amendments viz: strike out the words within [brackets] and insert those printed in *italics*.

Joint Resolution

[proposing amendments to the Constitution of the [United States] *submitting to the legislatures of the several states a proposition to amend the Constitution of the United States*

Be it resolved by the Senate and House of Representatives of the United States *of America* in Congress assembled, ~~two thirds of both Houses concurring therein~~ [That the following articles be proposed as amendments to the Constitution of the United States, which, when adopted by the Legislatures of three fourth of the several States, shall be valid to all intents and purposes as part of the said Constitution ~~hereof~~

Article 1. Slavery or involuntary servitude, except as a punishment for crime, shall not exist in the United States.

Article 2. The Congress whenever a majority of the members elected to each House, shall deem it necessary may propose amendments to the Constitution or on the application of ~~two thirds~~

18. Robert E. Lee's Acceptance of the Presidency of Washington College 1865

After the Civil War much of the nation was in ruin, but the South suffered the greatest losses because it had fought gallantly until it used all its strength and resources. Even General Robert E. Lee, commander of the Southern armies, had to find work. He was such a remarkably fair-minded gentleman that the North respected him and the South idolized him. Lee was offered several good business positions, but he turned them down because he wanted to do everything in his power to help rebuild his country.

Lee accepted the presidency of Washington College (it was named Washington and Lee after his death) because he felt it would give him the opportunity to teach what he believed, that "All should unite in honest efforts to obliterate the effects of war, and to restore the blessings of peace."

His letter says also, "I think it the duty of every citizen, in the present condition of the country, to do all in his power to aid in the restoration of peace and harmony."

in the present Condition of the Country, to do all in his power to aid in the restoration of peace & harmony, & in no way to oppose the policy of the State & Genl Governments, directed to that object. It is particularly incumbent on those charged with the instruction of the young, to set them an example of submission to authority, & I could not consent to be the cause of animadversion upon the College.

Should you however take a different view, & think that my services in the position tendered me by the Board will be advantageous to the College & Country, I will yield to your judgment & accept it. Otherwise I must most respectfully decline the office.

Begging you to express to the trustees of the College my heartfelt gratitude for the honor Conferred upon me, & requesting you to accept my Cordial thanks for the kind manner in which you have Communicated its decision,

I am Gentl with great respect
your most Obt Servt
R E Lee

Messrs John W. Brockenbrough Rector
S. McD Reid; Alfred Leyburn
Horatio Thompson, S. Bolivar Christian } Committee
J. J. Kirkpatrick

36

19.   Theodore Roosevelt's Letter on Cuba 1907

In 1898, Cuba, a small island south of the tip of Florida, wanted her independence from Spain. The United States joined Cuba in her fight for freedom and won the war.

When the Spanish-American War ended, the United States declared that it had no intention of controlling Cuba. The island was now free from Spain and should govern herself. But eight years later Cuba was again in trouble and called upon the United States for help.

The president of Cuba asked for United States troops to protect his government from being overthrown by rebel forces. President Theodore (Teddy) Roosevelt sent an investigating committee headed by Secretary of War William H. Taft. Strife and fear of the rebels grew so great on the island that the Cuban president resigned, and the newly elected congress did not assemble.

There was no legal government in Cuba. Now, President Roosevelt sent 7,500 marines to see that law and order were kept on the island. He sent a message to the Congress of the United States saying he had not wished to interfere in Cuba. He said that the United States had no intention of being a protector of Cuba indefinitely. U.S. marines would get out of the country as soon as the Cuban people were able to restore peace and an orderly government of their own.

In the letter you see here, written some months later to William Taft, Roosevelt once more emphasizes that the United States promised to leave Cuba as soon as its government could handle its own problems and it would do so—even though a portion of the Cuban people wanted a United States protectorate under which they would feel safer.

"The good faith of the United States," wrote Theodore Roosevelt, "is a mighty valuable asset and must not be impaired."

37

January 22, 1907.

My dear Mr. Secretary:

In reference to Magoon's two letters of the 13th and 16th, which are returned herewith, I need hardly add to what I said this morning.   There can be no talk of a protectorate by us.   Our business is to establish peace and order on a satisfactory basis, start the new government, and then leave the Island; the Cuban Government taking the reins into its own hands; tho of course it might be advisable for some little time that some of our troops should stay in the Islands to steady things.   I will not even consider the plan of a protectorate, or any plan which would imply our breaking our explicit promise because of which we were able to prevent a war of devastation last fall.   The good faith of the United States is a mighty valuable asset and must not be impaired.

Sincerely yours,

Theodore Roosevelt

Hon. Wm. H. Taft,
    Secretary of War.

20. Nineteenth Amendment (Civil Rights for Women) 1920

In 1848, members of a convention of women in Seneca Falls, N. Y., declared that women should have the right to vote. Most men laughed at the idea. Other men were angry. Men said that women were wonderful in their place, but their place was in the home as wives and mothers. Men shook their heads at the very idea that females could ever understand politics well enough to vote. And if women did vote, might it not turn their heads so that they would neglect their duties in the home?

Many women answered the laughter and anger by joining one of the organizations headed by three determined women working tirelessly for woman suffrage (the right to vote) : Elizabeth Cady Stanton, Susan B. Anthony and Lucy Stone. These women endured public humiliation and even prison to fight for equal rights for women and men.

In 1878 an amendment to give women the right to vote was written by Susan B. Anthony and sent to the Senate. This amendment, the nineteenth, was proposed to Congress every single year from 1878 to 1919 before it was finally approved and sent to the states for ratification.

During these years the women's groups had worked hard. In fifteen states women had already been granted the right to vote. Now they set out to gain the vote of twenty-one more states required to ratify the Nineteenth Amendment. In 1919, thirty-five states had ratified, but one more was needed. The next year, 1920, Tennessee gave its vote to the women. The amendment was the law of the land.

More than seventy years were required to secure the rights of women. Since then, in half that time, women have justified the trust in them. They not only vote, but many women hold political office or responsible jobs. They care for their homes and families as well.

Sixty-sixth Congress of the United States of America;

At the First Session,

Begun and held at the City of Washington on Monday, the nineteenth day of May, one thousand nine hundred and nineteen.

JOINT RESOLUTION

Proposing an amendment to the Constitution extending the right of suffrage to women.

Resolved by the Senate and House of Representatives of the United States of America in Congress assembled (two-thirds of each House concurring therein), That the following article is proposed as an amendment to the Constitution, which shall be valid to all intents and purposes as part of the Constitution when ratified by the legislatures of three-fourths of the several States.

"ARTICLE ————.

"The right of citizens of the United States to vote shall not be denied or abridged by the United States or by any State on account of sex.

"Congress shall have power to enforce this article by appropriate legislation."

F. H. Gillett

Speaker of the House of Representatives.

Thos. R. Marshall

Vice President of the United States and
President of the Senate.

40

21. Selection of Eisenhower as Supreme Commander of "Overlord" 1943

World War II, which began in Europe in September 1939, spread throughout the world. Hitler's Nazi Germany, with Italy and Japan, conquered most of Western Europe. Germany occupied France. Only the English Channel lay between the German army and England. Ripped and battered by constant air attacks, England stood alone against the Nazis.

Since the German and Italian dictators believed in the overthrow of all democratic freedoms, the sympathy of the United States was with England and France and their allies. Through Lend-Lease, the United States supplied the Allies with airplanes, ships and weapons. Communist Russia, under the dictator Stalin, did not declare herself. Then the Nazis attacked Russia. By Russia's act of fighting Germany, she also was on the side of the Allies.

The island of Japan had too many people and needed land desperately. Japan thought this was a good time to take for herself the Philippines and other Pacific islands which were under the protection of the United States. In a sneak attack at Pearl Harbor, Japan crippled a large part of the United States' Pacific Fleet and killed thousands of servicemen. From that hour, the United States, too, was in World War II on the side of the Allies.

Meanwhile Russia had been fighting Germany desperately, but the Germans marched deeper and deeper into Russian territory. Russia insisted that the Allies help her by attacking Germany on the French side, "a second front."

"Overlord" was the code name of the secret invasion plan made by the combined staffs of the United States and England. They planned to attack on a large scale the German army which occupied France. After the final meeting to discuss "Overlord," President Franklin D. Roosevelt wrote a quick note to the Russian dictator, Stalin, to tell him that General Eisenhower had been selected to head the invasion. Roosevelt signed the note.

At the bottom of the note is another note. It was written by General George Marshall to tell Eisenhower that he could keep this rough draft as a memento. (A typed official copy was probably sent to Stalin.)

41

From the President to Marshal Stalin

immediate
1. The appointment of your Eisenhower to command of Overlord operation has been decided upon.

Roosevelt

Cairo, Dec. 7. 43

Dear Eisenhower, I thought you might like to have this as a memento. It was written personally by me as the final meeting broke up yesterday, the President signing it immediately.

W.S.C.

22. Agreement for Invasion of Western Europe 1943

World War II was fought differently from any previous war. The speed of airplanes, boats and radio messages made great distances seem shorter and shorter. The heads of warring nations actually left their countries and met together with their allies to discuss, in person, the conduct of the war. At a meeting in Quebec, Prime Minister Churchill of England and President Franklin D. Roosevelt decided upon a plan to invade Western Europe at Normandy, France. They called the plan "Overlord." Later, at Teheran, the capital of Iran, Roosevelt and Churchill met with Stalin, the dictator of Russia. They decided upon the probable time of invasion. They also agreed to launch a supporting invasion, "Anvil," against the German army occupying Southern France.

The paper you see here was written to assure Stalin of the actual time of the invasion. At the top of the page, Roosevelt made corrections in red pencil in his own handwriting, "during the month of May." The rewrite at the end of the note is a correction in pencil written by Admiral Leahy, the President's Chief of Staff.

This is evidence of how carefully the men in official positions correct and rewrite papers so that the words say exactly what is meant. Read the original words of this note (crossed out). Now read the corrected words written in pencil. Did you notice that *simultaneously* had been crossed out? The word *simultaneously* meant that the attack on Southern France ("Anvil") would occur at the *same time* as the main attack, "Overlord." Since this might not be possible, Admiral Leahy rewrote the agreement, promising a supporting attack, without naming the time.

43

Agreed:-

To inform Stalin that we
will launch OVERLORD by June 1st,
~~and will simultaneously make~~
~~the biggest attack on Southern~~
~~France that is permitted by~~
~~the landing craft available~~
~~at that time.~~

during " The month"
May and

in ~~conjunction~~
~~together~~ with a supporting
operation in Southern France
of the largest ~~scale~~ that
is permitted by the landing
craft available at that
time

44

23. McAuliffe's Christmas Message 1944

Brigadier General McAuliffe's famous Christmas message to his trapped men needs little explanation. The letter is clearly typewritten. Read every word of it. Read it and be proud that there are men like this who fought for our country such a short time ago. One of them may be your father or uncle or neighbor.

On Christmas Eve, 1944, the 101st Airborne Division of the American army was surrounded by the enemy at Bastogne, Belgium. A map of the section hung in officers' quarters. It showed an unbroken ring of red marks around the American camp. Each red mark stood for a strong German division stationed at that point. It seemed as if the Americans faced certain death unless they surrendered. From the German commander, Brigadier General Anthony McAuliffe had received a demand to surrender.

General McAuliffe sat down and wrote a Christmas letter to his trapped troops. He told the men how serious their position was. He told them *why* they must continue to hold it.

He quoted the entire German demand that he and his forces surrender, and he wrote his own answer to the Germans in one word:

NUTS!

45

HEADQUARTERS 101ST AIRBORNE DIVISION
Office of the Division Commander

24 December 1944

What's Merry about all this, you ask? We're fighting - it's cold, we aren't home. All true but what has the proud Eagle Division accomplished with its worthy comrades of the 10th Armored Division, the 705th Tank Destroyer Battalion and all the rest? Just this: We have stopped cold everything that has been thrown at us from the North, East, South and West. We have identifications from four German Panzer Divisions, two German Infantry Divisions and one German Parachute Division. These units, spearheading the last desperate German lunge, were headed straight west for key points when the Eagle Division was hurriedly ordered to stem the advance. How effectively this was done will be written in history; not alone in our Division's glorious history but in World history. The Germans actually did surround us, their radios blared our doom. Their Commander demanded our surrender in the following impudent arrogance.

December 22nd 1944

"To the U. S. A. Commander of the encircled town of Bastogne.

The fortune of war is changing. This time the U. S. A. forces in and near Bastogne have been encircled by strong German armored units. More German armored units have crossed the river Ourthe near Ortheuville, have taken Marche and reached St. Hubert by passing through Hombres-Sibret-Tillet. Libramont is in German hands.

There is only one possibility to save the encircled U. S. A. Troops from total annihilation: that is the honorable surrender of the encircled town. In order to think it over a term of two hours will be granted beginning with the presentation of this note.

If this proposal should be rejected one German Artillery Corps and six heavy A. A. Battalions are ready to annihilate the U. S. A. Troops in and near Bastogne. The order for firing will be given immediately after this two hour's term.

All the serious civilian losses caused by this Artillery fire would not correspond with the well known American humanity.

The German Commander

The German Commander received the following reply:

22 December 1944

"To the German Commander:

N U T S !

The American Commander

Allied Troops are counterattacking in force. We continue to hold Bastogne. By holding Bastogne we assure the success of the Allied Armies. We know that our Division Commander, General Taylor, will say: "Well Done!"

We are giving our country and our loved ones at home a worthy Christmas present and being privileged to take part in this gallant feat of arms are truly making for ourselves a Merry Christmas.

McAULIFFE,
Commanding.

46

24. German Instrument of Surrender 1945

The surrender of all Nazi forces "on land, sea and in the air" was signed by the German High Command on May 7, 1945, at General Eisenhower's headquarters at Rheims. The next day another meeting took place in Berlin, where final surrender papers were signed. Victory in Europe was official on May 8, 1945.

Actually the end of the German war could be predicted in April when General Mark Clark announced that the British 8th Army and the American 5th Army had defeated the Nazis in Italy and forced a general German retreat. The Germans, too, realized that they were beaten. In early May, their commanders on the Western front begged the Allied Forces, made up of American and English troops and their Western allies, to allow the German troops to surrender only to the Allied Forces. The Germans did not want

Only this text in English is authoritative

ACT OF MILITARY SURRENDER

1.   We the undersigned, acting by authority
of the German High Command, hereby surrender
unconditionally to the Supreme Commander, Allied
Expeditionary Force and simultaneously to the
Soviet High Command all forces on land, sea, and in
the air who are at this date under German control.

2.   The German High Command will at once
issue orders to all German military, naval and
air authorities and to all forces under German
control to cease active operations at 2301 hours
Central European time on 8 May   and to
remain in the positions occupied at that time. No
ship, vessel, or aircraft is to be scuttled, or any
damage done to their hull, machinery or equipment.

3.   The German High Command will at once
issue to the appropriate commanders, and ensure
the carrying out of any further orders issued by
the Supreme Commander, Allied Expeditionary Force
and by the Soviet High Command.

4.   This act of military surrender is without
prejudice to, and will be superseded by any
general instrument of surrender imposed by, or
on behalf of the United Nations and applicable
to GERMANY and the German armed forces as a whole.

- 1 -

2

the Russian Red Army to have anything to do with their surrender or the peace terms. But Field Marshal Montgomery knew that all the nations fighting against Germany had agreed never to make a separate peace, so he refused.

The Allies waited two full days, after the Germans offered to surrender on the Western front, until arrangements could be made for the Germans fighting on the Russian front to surrender, too.

When we look at this paper of surrender, we must remember how near the Nazis came to destroying human freedoms. The Nazi domination began as an idea so small that many people laughed at those who knew and feared its growing power. Finally the Nazi idea caused the most terrible war the world has ever known. The lesson is clear. We must always be watchful for any "idea" which could take our freedoms from us.

49

5.   In the event of the German High Command
or any of the forces under their control failing
to act in accordance with this Act of Surrender,
the Supreme Commander, Allied Expeditionary Force
and the Soviet High Command will take such punitive
or other action as they deem appropriate.

Signed at *Rheims at 0241* on the   7th   day of May, 1945.
France

On behalf of the German High Command.

Jodl

IN THE PRESENCE OF

On behalf of the Supreme Commander,   On behalf of the Soviet
Allied Expeditionary Force.   High Command.

W. B. Smith   *Souslaparov*

F. Sevez -2-

Major General, French Army
            (Witness)

50

25. Instrument of Surrender in the Pacific 1945

Germany surrendered in May. The war in Europe was ended, but the war in the Pacific against the Japanese continued three more months. On September 2, 1945, on the deck of the battleship *Missouri* anchored in Tokyo Bay, General Douglas MacArthur accepted the surrender of Japan.

Immediately following the signing of the Tokyo papers, the Japanese armies gave themselves up to the Allied commanders on the many different islands where they had been fighting. Thus there are a number of Japanese papers of surrender. Some of these papers are single pages, some are longer. Some are printed and others typed. Some are on parchment paper, others on ordinary writing paper. All state the same terms: unconditional surrender.

When we look at the Instrument of Surrender in the Pacific, we should also remember that, at the beginning of the war, many brave American men were forced to surrender to the Japanese. The United States was so poorly prepared when Japan attacked her at Pearl Harbor that she could not go to the defense of her helpless fighting men in the Pacific.

General Jonathan Wainwright directed the defense of the Philippines in the early days of the war. He and his men fought longer than anyone believed they could. Finally, from Corregidor, General Wainwright sent a last message to the President of the United States: "There is a limit to human endurance and that limit has long since been passed. Without prospects of relief, I feel it is my duty . . . to end this useless effusion of blood and human sacrifice. . . . May God bless and preserve you and guide you and the nation in the effort to ultimate victory. With profound regret and continued pride in my gallant troops, I go to meet the Japanese Commander. Goodbye, Mr. President."

After his final message, General Wainwright and his troops endured the pain of seeing the American flag hauled down and surrendered to an enemy for the first time in the history of the nation.

General Wainwright lived through the years in a Japanese prison. He was released in time to witness the signing of the Tokyo papers after the "ultimate victory." Following the Tokyo signing, he was flown to the Philippines to witness the signing of the Instrument of Surrender there.

51

Instrument of Surrender

of the

Japanese and Japanese-Controlled Armed Forces in the Philippine Islands

to the

Commanding General

United States Army Forces, Western Pacific

Camp John Hay
Baguio, Mountain Province,
Luzon, Philippine Islands

3 September 1945

Pursuant to and in accordance with the proclamation of the Emperor of Japan accepting the terms set forth in the declaration issued by the heads of the Governments of the United States, Great Britain and China on 26 July 1945, at Potsdam and subsequently adhered to by the Union of Soviet Socialist Republics; and to the formal instrument of surrender of the Japanese Imperial Government and the Japanese Imperial General Headquarters signed at Tokyo Bay at 0908 on 2 September 1945:

1. Acting by command of and in behalf of the Emperor of Japan, the Japanese Imperial Government and the Japanese Imperial General Headquarters, We hereby surrender unconditionally to the Commanding General, United States Army Forces, Western Pacific, all Japanese and Japanese-controlled armed forces, air, sea, ground and auxiliary, in the Philippine Islands.

2. We hereby command all Japanese forces wherever situated in the Philippine Islands to cease hostilities forthwith, to preserve and save from damage all ships, aircraft and military and civil property, and to comply with all requirements which may be imposed by the Commanding General, United States Army Forces, Western Pacific, or his authorized representatives.

3. We hereby direct the commanders of all Japanese forces in the Philippine Islands to issue at once to all forces under their command to surrender unconditionally themselves and all forces under their control, as prisoners of war, to the nearest United States Army Force Commander.

4. We hereby direct the commanders of all Japanese forces in the Philippine Islands to surrender intact and in good order to the nearest United States Army Force Commander, at times and at places directed by him, all equipment and supplies of whatever nature under their control.

5. We hereby direct the commanders of all Japanese forces in the Philippine Islands at once to liberate all Allied prisoners of war and civilian internees under their control, and to provide for their protection, care, maintenance and immediate transportation to places as directed by the nearest United States Army Force Commander.

6. We hereby undertake to transmit the directives as given in Paragraphs 1 through 5, above, to all Japanese forces in the Philippine Islands immediately by all means within our power, and further to furnish to the Commanding General, United States Army Forces, Western Pacific, all necessary Japanese emissaries fully empowered to bring about the surrender of Japanese forces in the Philippine Islands with whom we are not in contact.

7. We hereby undertake to furnish immediately to the Commanding General, United States Army Forces, Western Pacific, a statement of the designation, numbers, location and commanders of all Japanese armed forces, ground, sea or air, in the Philippine Islands.

8. We hereby undertake faithfully to obey all further proclamation, orders and directives deemed by the Commanding General, United States Army Forces, Western Pacific, to be proper to effectuate this surrender.

Signed at Camp John Hay, Baguio, Mountain Province, Luzon, Philippine Islands, at 1210 hours 3 September 1945:

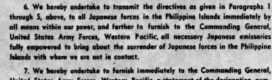

TOMOYUKI YAMASHITA,
General, Imperial Japanese Army
Highest Commander, Imperial
Japanese Army in the Philippines.

DENHICI OKOCHI,
Vice Admiral, Imperial Japanese Navy
Highest Commander, Imperial
Japanese Navy in the Philippines.

By command of and in behalf
of the Japanese Imperial
General Headquarters

Accepted at Camp John Hay, Baguio, Mountain Province, Luzon
Philippine Islands, at 1210 hours 3 September 1945:
For the Commander-in-Chief, United States Army Forces, Pacific:

EDMOND H. LEAVEY,
Major General, USA
Deputy Commander, United States Army Forces,
Western Pacific.

26.   United Nations Charter 1945

During World War II with its terrible cost in life and property, the wiser men of many nations realized that *something* must be done to prevent wars. In 1941, England's Prime Minister Churchill and President Franklin D. Roosevelt drew up a plan called the Atlantic Charter, which stated eight rules. The two leaders felt that if every nation would follow these rules, there was hope for peace in the world. Twenty-four nations soon signed these rules, which were called A Declaration of United Nations. As the war continued, more nations joined and signed with this group who wanted to end war forever.

At last, in April 1945, delegates, men and women from fifty nations, met together in San Francisco. They were to form a union and prepare a charter which they hoped would bring about peace and security. These men and women were still meeting when Germany surrendered. They knew that Japan must soon give up, but they kept working as hard as ever on the plan for the United Nations. They wanted to prevent war from ever happening again.

The charter was written and signed after long talks and hard work by the delegates to that convention, which continued from

(2) Each Government pledges itself to cooperate with the Governments signatory hereto and not to make a separate armistice or peace with the enemies.

The foregoing declaration may be adhered to by other nations which are, or which may be, rendering material assistance and contributions in the struggle for victory over Hitlerism.

Done at Washington
January First, 1942

The United States of America
by Franklin D Roosevelt

The United Kingdom of Great Britain
& Northern Ireland
by Winston S. Churchill

On behalf of the Government
of the Union of Soviet Socialist
Republics
Maxim Litvinov
(Ambassador)

National Government of the Republic of China
T.V. Soong
Minister for Foreign Affairs

The Commonwealth of Australia
by R.G. Casey

The Kingdom of Belgium
by Cte R. Straten

Canada
by Leighton McCarthy

April through June. Each of the fifty nations pledged itself to "settle international disputes by peaceful means."

Members of the United Nations realized that it must remain active and that countries must know and understand each other better, so they planned to have meetings. The charter established four main parts to the United Nations. 1. The Security Council, to enforce its principles. 2. The General Assembly, to discuss and debate problems. 3. The Economic and Social Council, to promote the welfare of countries. 4. The International Court of Justice.

Each of the fifty nations which signed the charter was given an exact copy of it. The United States bound the copy, photographed here, in blue morocco leather with the seal of the United Nations embossed in gold on its cover.

Many people believe that the United Nations Charter offers the world's only hope for peace. Learn all you can about the work of the United Nations in the years since this charter was signed. See if you agree. As you grow older, you must know what you believe—for *you* are needed to help keep the freedoms and peace in this world.

The Republic of Costa Rica
by Wm. Fernandez

The Republic of Cuba
by Aurelio F. Concheso.

Czechoslovak Republic
by V. S. Hurban

The Dominican Republic
by J Whonesio

The Republic of El Salvador
by C S Alfaro

The Kingdom of Greece
by Cimon G. Diamantopoulos.

The Republic of Guatemala
by Enrique Lopez Herrarte

La Republique d'Haiti
pour Fernand Dennis.

The Republic of Honduras
by Julián R Cáceres

India by
Girja Srankar Bajpai.

The Grand Duchy of Luxembourg
by Hugues Le Gallais

The Kingdom of the Netherlands
by Loudon

Signed on behalf of
the Govt of the Dominion
of New Zealand
by Frank Langstone

The Republic of Nicaragua
by Leon De Bayle

The Kingdom of Norway
by W. Munthe Morgenstierne

The Republic of Panamá
by A. Guardia

The Republic of Poland
by Jan Ciechanowski.

The Union of South Africa
by Ralph W. Close

The Kingdom of Yugoslavia
by Constantin A. Fotitch

56